WHAT OTHERS ARE SAYING

"The 7/24 challenge was a game changer for me. I grew up in the church and know the value of spending time in God's word.

When Hosea issued this challenge, I started my prayer each day with asking God to help me to listen slowly. This is a big deal for me as I am usually going a hundred miles an hour. To **listen slowly** *caused me to see this time not as a task to be completed but an opportunity to be still and hear God's voice speak through His Holy Spirit. I am a thinker so to* **think deeply** *resonated with me, but it also challenged me to journal my thoughts, dig deeper, and make application as I read God's word. Given the first two steps,* **praying fervently** *seemed natural as I interacted and conversed with God during our time together. The final step,* **obey faithfully**, *was new to me and yet the most important of all. It forced me to end my time with a heart of submission, a willingness to be obedient, a call for God to continue to transform me.*

I am grateful for the 7/24 challenge and Hosea's commitment to challenge a group of believers to enter into God's presence purposefully and humbly. I am forever changed."

- Dr. Jackie Minor - VEM Ministries

"Brother as you know I was born again while listening to you preach in 2001. In 2004 I met my beautiful wife. That being said I never got out of bed in the morning until I absolutely had to to make it to work sometimes a minute or two late. Then you brought up the 7/24 challenge and I told my wife, it's time for a change.

That was many years ago and I still to this day try my best to rise and spend time in my bible before I do anything else to start my day. It has made a big change in my life. Still have a ways to go but it changed my life for the better for sure. Thanks brother."

- Doug Browning

"In 2012 when I was about 22 and a young believer, I heard the 7/24 Challenge from Pastor Hosea. The challenge was simple to remember and follow. The consistent encouragement and accountability of the challenge helped me grow in digesting more of God's Word and obeying it. The challenge is highly reproducible and easily shared with others."

- Michael Wilbanks

WHAT OTHERS ARE SAYING (cont)

"Oh my goodness, I remember this! I would've been 14. I remember being thankful that this sounded like something special and practical that I could implement into my daily life. Any time that I get back into the Word after spending time away, I remind myself quality over quantity, and that mentality started with this challenge. So thankful for your obedience to the Holy Spirit!"
- Emilee Miller

"The 7/24 Challenge and the underlying principles that accompany it have made a significant difference in my devotional life and in my ability to hear and apply God's Word to my life. The daily discipline necessary to "build my house upon the rock" is certainly part of the benefit of the challenge. However, the 4 principles: Listen Slowly, Thnk Deeply, Pray Fervently and Obey Faithfully have given me a new focus and a new freedom. I now approach my Bible study with greater expectation that the Holy Spirit will reveal a truth or give me an insight into Scripture or into myself that I need to consider and to put into practice in my life. The challenge for me, in regard to Bible study, has become not to read more, but to listen better."
- Tom Coay

"Several years ago, my wife and I were looking for a home church for us and our three children.Friends of ours had suggested Ridgecrest Baptist Church numerous times mentioning the children's program and worship music. I had currently been struggling with our marriage and being a father. A few years earlier we lost my wife's father during the pregnancy of our first child. And about the year or so before attending Ridgecrest we lost my father. I found myself at a loss on how to be a good father and husband, and it left me feeling defeated and needing help.
One Sunday we were sitting in church and I heard the pastor read Matthew 7:24. "Everyone then who hears these words of mine and does them will be like a wise man who built his house on the rock.". He then talked about the 724 challenge. He asked, "Do you pray? Do you pray with your children, do you pray over your children, do you pray for your wife, do you pray over your wife, do you share God's word with your family?" The answer for me to those questions was sometimes, not always and never. In that moment I believe God spoke to me giving me a clear and simple way to be prepared as a husband and as a father. So I put it into practice. It seemed odd to try, but I instantly saw my family respond to the love that was being shared in those moments of prayer and in God's word together as a family. I've noticed over the years that it gets rid of the animosity that shows up in marriage sometimes. *(continued next page)*

WHAT OTHERS ARE SAYING (cont)

It's a place where I can let go of my bitterness, selfishness, or self-righteousness and just let my love be kind. That has had the greatest healing effect on my marriage, which makes us better parents together. And even though three kids tend to shut you out from time to time they always listen in those moments. I pray this is something that will always be practiced in my life. It has shown me the love of our heavenly Father and has been a guide in my journey as a father and husband."

- Michael Burgess

THE 7/24 CHALLENGE

BY HOSEA BILYEU

Scripture quotations marked (NLT) are taken from The Holy Bible, New Living Translation, copyright ©1996, 2004, 2007by Tyndale House Foundation. Used by permission of Tyndale House Publishers, Inc., Carol Stream, IL 60188. All rights reserved.

Scripture quotations marked NKJV are taken from the New King James Version ®. Copyright © 1982 by Thomas Nelson, Inc. Used by permission. All rights reserved.

Scripture quotations marked ESV are taken from The Holy Bible, English Standard Version ® (ESV®), copyright © 2001 by Crossway, a publishing ministry of Good News Publishers. Used by permission. All rights reserved.

View other resources from this author, including video lessons for this book by visiting online: www.hoseabilyeu.com

© 2020 Hosea Bilyeu

ISBN: 978-1-7356388-1-2

Hosea Bilyeu
503 North Ellen Street
Nixa, Missouri 65174
www.hoseabilyeu.com

CONTENTS

INTRODUCTION

"How are you doing, brother?" I asked, just after the end of our worship service.

"Couldn't be better, Pastor!" he replied with a smile.

I leaned up against the platform and listened as he continued.

"Well, there are some tough things going on now," he said, and he proceeded to tell me of some incredible challenges being faced by family and friends.

His next words warmed my heart and encouraged me greatly.

"A few weeks ago, I was having my 7/24 time and I was reading in Corinthians about how God's grace is sufficient for us. You know, Pastor, that is really true!" I sensed the strength and the joy of the Holy Spirit in his words and on his face.

How this man, young in the faith, came to such a mature perspective is the subject of this book. Why do some people grow in their relationship to God, while others do not seem to do so? Why do some go from strength to strength while others falter and sometimes fall away from their commitments to Christ? Why do so many of our young men and young ladies opt out of the Church and turn away from their faith in Christ when they leave high school? Why do so many of their parents walk away from the work of the Kingdom when their children are grown? Why do so many "good Christians" behave so badly?

Add to these questions this one: Why is a biblical worldview so rare among church-going people? A March 6, 2009 story on the Barna Group website tells of how a nationwide survey conducted by the Barna Group among a representative sample of adults explored how many have what might be considered a "biblical worldview." The report compared 2009 results from similar surveys conducted in 1995, 2000, and 2005.

For the purposes of the survey, a "biblical worldview" was defined as believing that absolute moral truth exists; the Bible is totally accurate in all of the principles it teaches; Satan is considered to be a real being or force, not merely symbolic; a person cannot earn their way into Heaven by trying to be good or by doing good works; Jesus Christ lived a sinless life on earth; and God is the all-knowing, all-powerful creator of the world who still rules the universe today. In the research, anyone who held all of those beliefs was said to have a biblical worldview. (I question why the physical resurrection of Christ or the Lordship of Christ are not on his list, but his research is still revealing.)

Overall, the research revealed that only 9% of all American adults have a biblical worldview. Among the sixty subgroups of respondents that the survey explored was one defined by those who said they have made a personal commitment to Jesus Christ that is important in their life today and that they are certain that they will go to Heaven after they die only because they confessed their sins and accepted Christ as their savior. Labeled "born again Christians," the study discovered that they were twice as likely as the average adult to possess a biblical worldview. However, that meant that even among born again Christians, less than one out of every five (19%) had such an outlook on life.

Every study I read strongly suggests that, when it comes to the moral and ethical issues of our day, professing Christians as a whole are not appreciably different from those who claim no faith in Christ, and in some cases are actually doing less well!

Is there anything that can change our trajectory? The answer is **Yes**! And, perhaps not surprisingly, the answer is not something new, but a return to something ancient, something that has been tried and proven true for millennia. Listen to the first song in the hymnbook of ancient Israel:

Blessed is the man who walks not in the counsel of the ungodly, nor stands in the path of sinners, nor sits in the seat of the scornful; But his delight is in the law of the Lord, and in His law he meditates day and night. He shall be like a tree planted by the rivers of water, that brings forth its fruit in its season, whose leaf also shall not wither; and whatever he does shall prosper.

Psalm 1:1-3 NKJV

This book is about meeting God in His Word, day by day and face to face, in such a way that we experience His transforming work in our lives. It is not about the **only** spiritual discipline God uses to change us, but it is about the **one** from which all other disciplines flow. My prayer is that God will use the 7/24 Challenge to radically reorient your life around Jesus Christ, so that you will join a growing number of followers of Christ who are striving for Christ-centered lives, seven days a week!

Are you ready for a challenge?

1.

ROCKY

It ain't about how hard you can hit;
it's about how hard you can get hit and keep moving forward.
Rocky Balboa

Rocky Balboa is a fictional character created by Sylvester Stallone and introduced to the world through six movies spread over 30 years. Two spin-off sequels followed in 2015 and 2018. Stallone describes his motivation by saying: *I relished stories of heroism, great love, dignity, and courage, dramas of people rising above their stations, taking life by the throat and not letting go until they succeeded.* The story of the making of the first movie seems to parallel the drama itself. The film, made for only $1.1 million and shot in 28 days, was a sleeper hit; it made over $117.2 million, the highest grossing film of 1976 for the US, and won three Oscars, including Best Picture (information from *Wikipedia*).

If you had a nickname spiritually, what would it be? Would people call you "Kid" because you have never grown up? Would they call you "Shaky," because you lack stability? Would your nickname be "Sleepy, Sneezy, Dopey, Doc, Happy, Bashful, or Grumpy?" Or would people call you "Rocky," because no matter how hard you are hit, you get up and keep moving forward?

I never remember not singing. I was the youngest of nine children, raised on a farm in a home without television, and much of our entertainment was centered around the songs of our faith. I am amazed by how many of the songs learned as a child are still in my memory today!

Often those songs were accompanied by hand or body movements that served to anchor them even deeper in my mind.

The wise man built his house upon the rock, we sang (while putting fist over fist and then forming a house and a rock). But there was also the foolish man who built his house on the sand, leading me to my favorite moment in the song: *and the house on the sand went "SPLAT!"* Even then I had little compassion for a fool (unless, of course, I was the fool)! It was a child's song with a grown-up message, and it came from the Bible.

At the end of the Sermon on the Mount, in Matthew 7:24-27, we find these powerful words from the lips of our Lord:

"Therefore whoever hears these sayings of Mine, and does them, I will liken him to a wise man who built his house on the rock: and the rain descended, the floods came, and the winds blew and beat on that house; and it did not fall, for it was founded on the rock.

But everyone who hears these sayings of Mine, and does not do them, will be like a foolish man who built his house on the sand: and the rain descended, the floods came, and the winds blew and beat on that house; and it fell. And great was its fall." NKJV

The first verses above describe the life I want to live. I want to be a Rocky! I want to weather the storms of life in such a way that God gets the glory and the world gets a witness.

Let's begin with some observations. First, this parable clearly indicates that there are people who are wise and there are people who are foolish. It may not be politically correct to say so, but it is still true. The question is, which are you? Which am I?

A second observation is simply that hard times come whether you are wise or foolish! The rain comes, the floods rise, trouble comes to all. But please notice one magnificent difference: Those who are wise build lives that will stand every test, including death itself! The foolish people are building lives on sand, lives that will ultimately fail.

Now, back to a central question: Am I a wise man or a foolish man? Are you a wise man, a wise woman, or are you living foolishly? Please understand, if you are without Christ, you are without God and without hope (see Ephesians 2:12). *The fool has said in his heart, there is no God* (Psalm 14:1 NKJV). I want to tell you, lost man or woman, boy or girl, your days are numbered, and you are not living wisely if you are leaving Jesus out!

But what if you are a believer in Christ? Is it possible to be a born-again believer and still be living foolishly? Absolutely! This is not to doubt our salvation, but it is to examine how well we are using our lives for His glory. So how can we live wisely?

The text gives us two necessities for wise living. First, wise living is only possible if we are **hearing** the words of Jesus (the Word of God). This is not just on an occasional basis but is a continual reality. It is larger than simply reading or hearing Scripture, it is hearing the voice of God through His Word. I will hear God most clearly when I am saturating my life in His Word.

It is a good time for us to pause and ask: Am I continually hearing the voice of God through His Word? I believe this is part of wise living, a significant part of what it means to build our houses - our lives - on the rock.

The second necessity, according to Jesus, is that we are **doing** what Jesus says. A disciple is not just informed; a disciple is transformed, and that transformation comes through obeying God's Word. I must be continually hearing the voice of God through His Word, but I must also be consistently obeying the word I have heard. Too often we are guilty of what Dallas Willard referred to as the "great omission from the great commission." We fail to become true apprentices of Jesus who practice what He practiced! Remember what Jesus said? *Teaching them to* ***observe*** *all things* (Matthew 28:20; emphasis added). We are too often satisfied with hearing that falls short of obedience!

Please notice how both of these are necessary if we are to be wise builders. To say, "I will do what Jesus said," while ignoring His Word is hypocrisy of the worst kind, and to say, "I will hear His Word," without a commitment to obedience is presumption of the worst kind! **We must live in the word and we must live by the word** if we are to live in true wisdom!

In the first months of 2009 I was in a pattern in my life in the Word exemplified by fitful starts and stops. Don't misunderstand me: I have loved God's Word for many years and have memorized scripture (at times) and meditated on it. I have preached for decades, and I was spending time weekly in the Word. However, my personal "face time" with God was sporadic. I looked back at my notes and found this pattern:

Spent time seeking God in His Word, January 1,
2009; missed January 2;
back in the word on
January 3; missed the
4th; etc., etc. etc.!

But God touched my heart between January 1 and April 7, and He used the words of Jesus in Matthew 7:24 as a catalyst for my change. For well over a decade I have been living in God's word, seeing my appetite for God increase, and experiencing life-change in fresh ways. My prayer is that I will never miss a day in His Word until I see the face of my Lord! (I do, however, miss days on occasion, and I do not condemn myself when I do.) I have shared with my family that if I am ever incapacitated to the point that I cannot read God's Word, I want them to put earphones on me and let me listen to Scripture or read to me from God's Word every day. I am serious! This is life to me! (Then they are to pipe great gospel music into my brain, and if I don't move, unplug me!)

This brings me to what I believe is one of the most significant teachings in my ministry. I bring to you a challenge, one that I call the **7/24 Challenge**. Here it is:

7 days a week I will spend at least 24 minutes each day interacting with God through His Word.

I am sure you noticed: the 7/24 Challenge derives its name from Matthew 7:24. This is not a new legalism; it is an invitation to liberty! This is not a way to get Jesus to love you more, it is a way to spend time with the One who loved you and gave Himself for you! It is your "face time" with the faithful Lover of your soul!

You may be thinking, "Given my circumstances, this is impossible." It is not about our circumstances; it is about our choices. If it feels like an elephant-sized commitment, eat it one bite at a time. How about 12 minutes, twice each day? How about six minutes, 4 times each day? This challenge is asking us for 1 minute out of each hour of our life! By the way, Shayla Hale, then Childhood Minister at Ridgecrest Baptist Church in Springfield, Missouri, suggested a modification for younger children: **I will spend 7 minutes out of every 24 hours interacting with God through His word.** That works!

You might say, "Pastor, I don't know how to do this!" In this book I will be carefully teaching you how to hear and respond to God's voice. Never forget that your purpose is communion with your Father! Out of that communion comes the power to live Christ-centered lives, seven days a week.

But, before we move to specific helps and suggestions to maximize your time in God's Word, let's think through the critical issue of preparation.

2.

A PREPARED HEART

The writer of Hebrews addresses the reality that God's Word exposes our spiritual condition. In Hebrews 4:11-13 we read:

For the word of God is living and powerful, and sharper than any two-edged sword, piercing even to the division of soul and spirit, and of joints and marrow, and is a discerner of the thoughts and intents of the heart. And there is no creature hidden from His sight, but all things are naked and open to the eyes of Him to whom we must give account. NKJV

Reading those words might suggest our best choice would be to run from the penetrating Word of God! It is true that God knows my name; it is also true that God knows my game! We cannot (and should not) hide from His sight. He is the Great Physician who can diagnose our spiritual diseases and prescribe a way of life that will bring healing.

Listen to what the writer said next:

Seeing then that we have a great High Priest who has passed through the heavens, Jesus the Son of God, let us hold fast our confession. For we do not have a High Priest who cannot sympathize with our weaknesses, but was in all points tempted as we are, yet without sin. Let us therefore come boldly to the throne of grace, that we may obtain mercy and find grace to help in time of need. (Hebrews 4:14-16 NKJV)

Isn't the love of God amazing! He sees us exactly as we are (and you know what I mean) and loves us anyway with an infinite, incredible love! Jesus is a sympathizing Savior! Even in our mess, we are called to His side, called to approach His throne; not with guilty fear and not with an arrogant spirit, but with a humble boldness because Jesus has opened the way for us to enter the throne room of God. We are not wise if we rush in "where angels fear to tread;" we are to come before God bowing our knees and confessing with our mouths that Jesus is Lord!

Let me say it clearly: If you are not a child of God, the Bible will be a mostly closed book to you! Paul speaks to the people in Corinth and to us with these words:

But the natural man does not receive the things of the Spirit of God, for they are foolishness to him; nor can he know them, because they are spiritually discerned.
(1 Corinthians 2:14 NKJV)

To hear from Heaven, to be guided by the good hand of God, we will have to make spiritual preparation, and that preparation starts with conversion! *You must be born again*, Jesus said to Nicodemus (John 3:7). How does that happen? Through the Word and by the Spirit! Indeed, the Father, the Son, and the Holy Spirit all work to bring us eternal life! God enables us to hear His Word, which calls us to repentance and faith (Romans 10:17); the Holy Spirit convicts us of *sin, and of righteousness, and of judgment* (John 16:8); the Father draws us to the Son (John 6:44); and His Son, Jesus Christ, saves us (Matthew 18:11)! If you have not experienced His saving grace in the forgiveness of your sins, and His assurance that you are one of His own, listen to His Word! Read the gospels, meet the Lord, and call on Him to save you (Romans 10:9-13)!

"I am already a Christian, Pastor. I have met Jesus, and He saved me! So do I still need to prepare to hear His voice?"

Yes! If we fail to make preparation, the noise in our lives and the noise in the world will drown out the whisper of God in our souls. We will be poor soil for the Word (see Matthew 13:18-23) and will fail to see spiritual fruit in our lives.

Here is what I mean: Before I go to bed, I have prepared the place where I will meet God in the morning. I have a comfortable chair; my iPad is charging beside it, and my notebook and pen are in place. When I first wake up in the morning, I direct my thoughts toward God. I "think a prayer" for Jesus to be exalted in my life, and I get up. Soon I am seated and I pause again for prayer, making sure I give time for the Holy Spirit to search my heart. Known sin needs to be confessed and forsaken; forgiveness needs to be claimed; and if there is relational junk left over from yesterday, I may need to pledge to do what I can to restore a relationship or release a hurt. Because I know that without the work of the Holy Spirit, I will not be able to hear God or understand what I read, I pray. I ask the Holy Spirit to be my teacher, to help me think clearly and hear well what God has to say to me. I pledge my obedience to the Word I will hear and ask for the Word to be planted deeply in my heart and life.

I can almost hear you saying, "That doesn't fit my schedule at all! I might as well give up before I start!" As teacher and author Steve Brown would say, "That is a lie from the pit of hell, and it smells like smoke."

It is not important that you "do it like Hosea;" it is important that you "do it!" Get creative with your time; identify timewasters in your life; look for times where you are waiting for someone or something. If you bring your desire and your will to this spiritual discipline, God will help you find a way when there seems to be no way.

This is a heart issue first; the time issue is a distant second Susanna Wesley (1669-1742) was the mother of nineteen children, nine of whom died in infancy. Among her surviving children were John Wesley and Charles Wesley, founders of the Methodist movement. Susanna homeschooled her children successfully through many trials, including persecution, her husband's imprisonment, sickness, and poverty. When she needed time alone with God, she simply pulled her apron over her head to pray. That was the children's signal to leave Mom alone! (This was taken from "Susanna's Apron" blog by Columba Lisa Smith.). Here is the bottom line: If you want to hear from God, prepare!

3.

LISTEN SLOWLY

This chapter and the next three are the nuts and bolts of the 7/24 Challenge. These take the concept of "interacting with God" and show how that can work day after day and year after year - always remaining fresh, and always producing spiritual fruit. The concepts are modified from an ancient practice, *Lectio Divina*, which was spiritual reading, meditation, and prayer intended to promote communion with God.

The first word in this chapter's title is "Listen." Your mind may go immediately to hearing God's Word spoken, whether by a preacher, a teacher, or someone else. These are all very helpful and recommended, but I am using the word differently, primarily as a contrast to just "reading the Bible." Sadly, many Christians make "reading the Bible" their goal and are happy to check off five more chapters or complete their reading of the whole Bible. Again, my purpose is not to discourage you from reading your Bible, but to change (if needed) your perspective. Your mission (if you choose to accept it!) is to hear from heaven, to hear what God has to say to you, personally, this very day. And this mission is most definitely possible. However, to hear from God through His word, you need to be in the "listening mode," not just a "reading mode." When we are in the "reading mode" we can easily find we have "read" a paragraph or a chapter in our Bible and have no idea what we just read! A disciplined mind, focused on hearing what God wants to say to you, can help prevent mindless reading and missed opportunities for hearing and growing.

This morning I "listened my way" through Psalm 21-23 and got some fresh words from God concerning the *unending blessings* (21:6) He has given me (I will live thankfully today!); the truth (22:19) that He **is** my strength (as opposed to simply **giving me** strength); and that I can live with courage – whatever comes – because *even though I walk through the darkest valley,* He is *with me* (23:4). In the words of hymn writer Philip P. Bliss, these are "wonderful words of life!"

That brings me to the second word in this chapter's title: "Slowly." When it comes to your Bible, speed reading can be dangerous to your spiritual health! I have come to the place where I believe how much I **hear** is more important than how much I **read**. I remember well a time in my ministry (I was in my early 30s) when I read the 6th chapter of Romans as part of a daily discipline. The next day, I felt prompted in my spirit to read the chapter again. As I recall, I spent about six weeks in Romans 6, and it truly got implanted into my life, bringing with it a new freedom in Christ.
These words became real to me then and are still dear to me now: *For sin shall not have dominion over you, for you are not under law, but under grace* (Romans 6:14). I put my name in that verse and named my sin in that verse, and watched the Spirit do a work in me! For those six weeks, I did not read much scripture, but through listening slowly the seed of the Word had time to germinate in my life and do the work God intended it to do. I do not believe this would have happened if I had felt compelled to read a certain number of verses or chapters.

Dallas Willard, in his book, *Hearing* God, says: “You may have been told that it is good to read the Bible through every year and that you can ensure this will happen by reading so many verses per day from the Old and New Testaments. If you do this you may enjoy the reputation of one who reads the Bible through each year, and you may congratulate yourself on it. But will you become more like Christ and more filled with the life of God? It is a proven fact that many who read the Bible in this way, as if they were taking medicine or exercising on a schedule, do not advance spiritually. **It is better in one year to have ten good verses transferred into the substance of our lives than to have every word of the Bible flash before our eyes.** Remember that "the letter kills, but the Spirit gives life" (2 Cor 3:6). We read to open ourselves to the Spirit.” (Page 163, emphasis added.)

I want to speak now to those of you who seldom read. Since you may not have read this book, someone else may be pointing this out to you for your encouragement! Can a person who learns in ways other than reading still make progress as a disciple of Jesus Christ? Absolutely! If you do not read (much), how about listening to scripture being read, and listening slowly? I simply mean hitting the pause button or turning off the recording to allow you to assimilate what you are reading (more about that in the next chapter). How about taking one scripture or short scripture passage, writing it on a card or in the Message app of your smart phone or tablet, and rereading it over and over all day long, meditating on and perhaps memorizing God’s word? If you are not where you can read or hear God’s Word, even a single verse, then practice setting your mind on Jesus Christ, because He truly is the Living Word! Finally, you can find collections of scripture songs and play them, allowing music to be used of God to open your heart and imprint His word in your mind.

Where do you start in your "slow listening" to God? If you are somewhat new to the Word, it is probably not the best idea to start in Genesis to read straight through the Bible. Perhaps you could try starting with the gospels (Matthew, Mark, Luke, and John), simply becoming better acquainted with Jesus and His teachings. From there, you might consider Acts, and then continue to read the rest of the New Testament. Indeed, you could profitably go back and read the Gospels again when you finish the New Testament.

By then you could go to the Old Testament and start with Genesis. The Book of Psalms and the Book of Proverbs can be used at any time and returned to often. Much wisdom comes from repeated times in those books. There are reading plans that involve reading five Psalms and one chapter from Proverbs each day, finishing both books in a month, but I still encourage you not to set "number of chapter" goals, at least not for a while. There will come a time in your spiritual walk where reading through the entire Bible may be wonderfully fulfilling and helpful. I am currently reading through one translation and then changing translations for the next reading. However, I am unconcerned about whether it takes me a year or much longer.

There are many great Bible reading plans available online. Most if not all Bible apps include plans to read scripture in a systematic way. Variety in your approach may be wise, so do not be afraid to try different plans. The final portion of this book will list resources that are helpful to many, and additional reading plans can be found on many of those sites.

"What do I listen for, Pastor? How can I expect God to speak to me?"

I'm glad you asked! Let me answer that from an objective standpoint, and then share more subjective thoughts that might be useful.

Paul was a seasoned ministry practitioner when he wrote to his younger protégé, Timothy, with these sound words (2 Tim 3:16-17):

All Scripture is inspired by God and is useful to teach us what is true and to make us realize what is wrong in our lives. It corrects us when we are wrong and teaches us to do what is right. God uses it to prepare and equip his people to do every good work.

When you and I are interacting with God through His Word, we are engaged with a book that is "God-breathed" (the literal meaning of *inspired*) and wonderfully profitable for us! We listen well if we listen for truth we need to embrace, error we need to shun, behaviors that are helpful and need to be practiced and behaviors that are hurtful and need to be rejected. Remember, listen slowly! **The outcome of good listening is good works accomplished for God's glory!**

More subjectively, as you read expect a verse or even a sentence to catch your attention or touch your heart. Expect an, "I need to hear this," awareness in your mind; it may well be the Holy Spirit urging you to slow down or stop. Follow those promptings! Every line of God's Word is inspired; God's Word is infallible and unfailing; but there will be certain truths that He will want you to see and seize as you read, and those words will become "living bread" to you. I have been helped by the wise words of author Marilyn McEntyre in her excellent book, *What's in a Phrase? Pausing Where Scripture Gives You Pause*. Every day as I listen slowly to God's Word, I often "push the pause button" when something touches my heart. I am reminded of the word *Selah*, found seventy-one times in the Psalms of the Bible. This may be a musical notation, or a call to pause for a moment. One writer said that every time we see the word *Selah* we should read it, "What do you think of that?" One of the things I am fond of saying is that people are not changed by sermons; they are changed by sentences.

Even when you listen to preaching, it is important for you to be alert to capture the sentence that could change your life.

Donald Grey Barnhouse talked about the need to give adequate time to our study of scripture. He said, "Read your Bible slowly. Take time, even if you have but little time. Give God the opportunity to talk back to you. This is the most important part of Bible study. When you merely plow through the Scriptures, letting your brain have full play over the text, making decisions as to what it means, and incorporating it into the corpus of your theology, it is comparatively worthless for spiritual results."

Listen to God's Word, listen for God's voice, and listen slowly!

4.

THINK DEEPLY

“The scandal of the evangelical mind is that there is not much of an evangelical mind.” These words came from one of evangelicalisms most respected historians, Mark Noll, in his 1991 book, *The Scandal of the Evangelical Mind*. To put it simply, we believers in Christ are not thinking enough or thinking deeply enough. We live on autopilot as we go about our days and weeks, seldom reflecting on anything that is happening to us, in us, through us, or around us.

This thinking deficit impacts us in many areas of our lives, but perhaps nowhere more significantly than in our time interacting with God through His word. Most of us can testify that it is possible to read the Bible without thinking much (or even at all) about what we are reading. However, this does not bring spiritual transformation to our lives. For that to happen, we need to **think deeply** concerning the revelation we are receiving from the Word.

Here’s what I mean: As I read my Bible, I come to a verse or passage that has a message I need. The Holy Spirit is active in helping me sense this, and I pause. I will often write in my notebook the sentence that arrested my attention (this also helps me **listen slowly**), and then reread it, perhaps several times. Then I lean back and **think**! Why did the Spirit prompt me to stop on this verse? What truth is there that I need?

What changes may I need to make in my thinking or in my living? This is meditation, a "chewing on the bone of truth" until I have tasted the marrow of the message God has for me. As thoughts come to mind, I will write them in my notebook for future pondering.

On July 14, 2012, I was interacting with God through His word. In Psalm 31:5 I found these words: *Into your hands I commit my spirit*. My mind jumped to the cross where Jesus died, the cross where He spoke His seven last sayings, including these same words employed by the Psalmist (see Luke 23:46). I stopped to think, mulling this over in my mind; and a thought I had never thought before occurred to me: This was not the first time Jesus had spoken these words! He was quoting scripture, and that scripture may well have been at the heart of Who He was and how He lived His life. Indeed, He lived all His life committing Himself to His Father. Hear His own words: *the Son can do nothing of Himself, but what He sees the Father do; for whatever He does, the Son also does in like manner* (John 5:19-20 NKJV). Every day He committed His spirit to God; and when the day of His death came, the day for which He came into the world, He died with the same words on his lips that he had lived by from the cradle to the cross. My time interacting with God through this Word yielded this sentence: **Our daily words will be our dying words!** The words I live by today (whether those are from God's Word or from the world's lies) will be the words I die by someday. I would be wise to choose carefully the words I am living by!

This insight (which is now part of who I am, implanted in my life) would not have come through a superficial reading of scripture. Deep truths must be mined by drilling down into the depths of God's Word. This takes time! Wisdom comes not from the microwave but from the simmering crock pot. *How sweet are Your words to my taste, Sweeter than honey to my mouth* (Ps 119:103 NKJV)! **Think deeply** and be satisfied!

Martin Luther King, Jr, said: *Rarely do we find men who willingly engage in hard, solid thinking. There is an almost universal quest for easy answers and half-baked solutions. Nothing pains some people more than having to think.*

If we would progress spiritually into the likeness of Christ, we must embrace the hard work of thinking that follows the reading or hearing of God's Word. Indeed, you might need to spend days or weeks on a single passage. Remain sensitive to the Holy Spirit's promptings and take as long as needed.

5.

PRAY FERVENTLY

Prayer has been a struggle for me. It is not that I don't pray; it is more that I struggle to understand prayer, and how to pray in accordance with God's will. Too often my praying seems lifeless, and I long to pray like Elijah – effectively and fervently!

The 7/24 Challenge is rescuing my prayer life from the doldrums. Every day that I meet the Father in His Word – listening slowly and thinking deeply – the stronger and more consistent I become in prayer.

Here's how it works: As I listen slowly to God's Word, some word, phrase, or sentence seems to invite my attention, and I hit the "pause button." I begin to think about the word or words that have arrested me, and to meditate on the implications of those words. Once I begin to discern how God is informing, inspiring, or correcting me through His word, I begin to pray. I pray God's Word back to Him! **Because I know what He has to say, I know what to say to Him.** In Psalm 27:8 (NKJV), we hear these words from David: *When You said, "Seek my face," my heart said to You, "Your face, Lord, I will seek."* In prayer, he said what God said, and prayed according to the will of God!

Recently I have been reading in Deuteronomy 2. In verse 31, God speaks to Moses concerning Sihon, the king of

Heshbon, an enemy of God's people: *"Look, I have begun to hand King Sihon and his land over to you. Begin now to conquer and occupy his land."* (NLT). I pushed the pause button on the last sentence and began to think of areas of my life still controlled by the world, the flesh, or the devil. I began to praise God for delivering me from bondage and confessed that I still struggled with besetting sins (Hebrews 12:1). I listened as He spoke to me through His word: *Begin now!* He knows how I procrastinate in areas of my life, and He addressed me and arrested me by His Word! I reflected on the word *conquer* and was reminded that there are no victories without a battle. I turned those thoughts back to God in prayer, asking Him to fight for me against my enemies. Finally, I wrestled with the words, *occupy his land*, and remembered that I can take back from the devil the things he has taken from me, but only through the empowerment of the Holy Spirit; and I asked for the filling of the Spirit so that I could not only win the battle, I could maintain the peace!

I have found that listening slowly and thinking deeply can *shape* my prayers as well. At the time of this writing, we have a granddaughter with some significant health needs. During the time I have been praying for her, I have also revisited the Model Prayer. As I pondered that prayer, I found myself praying like this: *Thy kingdom come, Thy will be done in earth* – in Ella Marie Bilyeu – *as it is in heaven* (Matthew 6:10 KJV).

Also, in listening to God speak through 1 John 3:2 in the New King James Version (*Beloved, now we are children of God; and it has not yet been revealed what we shall be, but we know that when He is revealed, we shall be like Him, for we shall see Him as He is.*), and in thinking deeply about the "now" and the "not yet," I am asking God to let the "not yet" break into the "now" of Ella's life, just as He has done countless times before! I am in no way seeking to manipulate the Father, but I am seeking to pray in accordance with scripture that He may have brought to my mind for such a time as this.

One final example of how listening slowly and thinking deeply is guiding my prayers comes from a recent rereading of Matthew 15:21-28 in the New Living Translation:

Then Jesus left Galilee and went north to the region of Tyre and Sidon. A Gentile woman who lived there came to him, pleading, "Have mercy on me, O Lord, Son of David! For my daughter is possessed by a demon that torments her severely." But Jesus gave her no reply, not even a word.

Then his disciples urged him to send her away. "Tell her to go away," they said. "She is bothering us with all her begging." Then Jesus said to the woman, "I was sent only to help God's lost sheep – the people of Israel." But she came and worshiped him, pleading again, "Lord, help me!" Jesus responded, "It isn't right to take food from the children and throw it to the dogs." She replied, "That's true, Lord, but even dogs are allowed to eat the scraps that fall beneath their masters' table." "Dear woman," Jesus said to her, "your faith is great. Your request is granted." And her daughter was instantly healed."

That was one stubborn lady! Jesus gave her ample opportunities to just give up and go home, but He wanted his disciples to see her willingness to persevere in her supplications for her daughter. How is this impacting my prayer life? I made a commitment to engage in "stubborn supplication" until my request is granted, or God shows me the prayer I should be praying! I also made a commitment to have a "surrendered soul," always praying as my Lord prayed in the Garden of Gethsemane: "Not as I will, but as you will." (Matthew 26:39 ESV)

Please remember: As we are listening slowly, thinking deeply, and praying fervently we are in the receiving mode, not the achieving mode. We are humbled and hungry before God, truly desiring to hear Him speak to us through His Word. His word is life!

6.

OBEY FAITHFULLY

It is tempting to say we have arrived at true discipleship – listening slowly to God speak through His word, thinking deeply concerning the word He has spoken, and praying fervently concerning our response to that word. However, it just isn't so! We can be practicing all those disciplines and still be falling short in terms of what it means to be an authentic follower of Jesus Christ.

Listen again to the text that prompted this journey I am on, and also prompted the writing of this guide:

"Therefore whoever hears these sayings of Mine, and does them, I will liken him to a wise man who built his house on the rock: and the rain descended, the floods came, and the winds blew and beat on that house; and it did not fall, for it was founded on the rock.

"But everyone who hears these sayings of Mine, and does not do them, will be like a foolish man who built his house on the sand: and the rain descended, the floods came, and the winds blew and beat on that house; and it fell. And great was its fall." NKJV

Notice again the similarities of the two hearers (they were both hearers). They both experienced life in all its complexity and mystery; one "house" fell; the other stood firm. The difference is in the foundation! The first made "hearing and doing" God's word his foundation; the second heard but failed to obey. The first foundation was obedience to the words of Jesus, the Rock of Ages! The second foundation was the sand of a man hearing without obeying. The first man was wise; the second was foolish.

This is the difference between reading your Bible for information and interacting with God through His word for transformation.

I fear many Christians relate to God's word with a "cafeteria" mentality: "I'll take this," "I'll pass on that." We think we can pick and choose what words of Christ we will obey, and in a sense we can. However, as is true with all choices, we cannot choose the consequences of our choices. If we fail to obey what we have heard, thought about, and prayed about, our lives are at risk! We are on shifting, changing sand, and disaster is not far ahead. But if we are *doers of the word and not hearers only* (James 1:22) we are on solid ground, and our lives will stand whatever test may come.

After teaching the 7/24 Challenge to a wonderful group of believers, a lady came to me with this thought: How about "Obey Immediately' as the fourth guideline? My answer? "That is awesome!" We should be obeying immediately, because when we fail to do so, we may not obey at all.

Someone has suggested that if we do not respond to new information or inspiration within seventy-two hours, the likelihood is that we will not do so at all. As for me, I want to always obey faithfully **and** immediately.

Beloved, hear me carefully: The journey of a disciple is not a never-ending upward curve of spiritual growth. Expect starts and stops; expect there to be days when you take more steps backward than forward; expect to still struggle with *every weight, and the sin which so easily ensnares* (Hebrews 12:1 NKJV). But know this: persistence on this path will still enable you to *run with endurance the race that is set before* (you) as you are continually *looking unto Jesus, the author and finisher of* (your) *faith* (Hebrews 12:1, 2 NKJV).

7.

THE DANGER OF DISCIPLINE

It may well be that the title of this chapter seems almost heretical! Doesn't everybody know the importance of spiritual disciplines? Dallas Willard, in his book *The Spirit of the Disciplines*, enumerates the disciplines of abstinence (solitude, silence, fasting, frugality, chastity, secrecy, and sacrifice) and the disciplines of engagement (study, worship, celebration, service, prayer, fellowship, confession, and submission). To paraphrase Dr. Willard, a spiritual discipline is an activity we can engage in now that will allow us to do later what we cannot do now by direct effort. "Spiritual disciplines enable us to do what needs to be done when it needs to be done" (Bill Gaultiere, soulshepherding.org blog).

So how could a spiritual discipline like the 7/24 Challenge be a danger? Any spiritual discipline has within it the possibility that we will begin to trust the discipline rather than the God who meets us and changes us as we practice that discipline! Indeed, we may become proud of our ability to "stick with it," and be condescending in our attitude toward those we see as "weaker" brothers or sisters. When this happens, Satan celebrates!

I like to think of spiritual disciplines as ditch-digging that will allow the water of life to flow into our souls. How foolish it would be for me to trust the ditch to do what only the water can do! As I spend face time through the Word with my heavenly Father day after day, delighting in the conversations we have, the transforming grace of God has easy access to my heart. But it is God who transforms my life, through His Spirit and His Word, in the context of a community of believers! I trust the triune God (Father, Son, and Holy Spirit) to form me into the image of Christ.

A second danger is that a person practicing the 7/24 Challenge might fall for the lie that it makes God love us more. This is a favorite strategy of the enemy, and sometimes works best on those who are most disciplined. However, it is not true! God loves you just as you are and just where you are! Nothing you do will make Him love you more, and nothing will make Him love you less. His love is one of the true constants in our ever-changing lives and circumstances.

A third danger, closely aligned with the first two, is simply the lure of legalism, with the corresponding assumption that we can somehow control what happens in our lives. The illogical thought is that if we will keep the rules, dot the i's and cross the t's, check off our list of things to do, God will behave in certain ways and our lives can be managed. That is an attractive and absolutely false philosophy of life. Those who practice such an approach to life will either be lifted up in pride or cast down in despair. We are to do what we do with due regard for our God, knowing that He is sovereign and that fearing Him and pleasing Him is true wisdom.

Let me mention one other danger: the danger of thinking "my way" is the only way. I have experienced life-change at a greater level since I began practicing the 7/24 Challenge. I know it has helped me. But I also know that everyone is different, and there may be other ways in which you can experience accelerated life-change. Dallas Willard, who is rejoicing in the presence of Jesus now, suggested that a "daily 'quiet time' is like trying to take a shower one drop at a time!" (Quoted by Bill Gaultiere, soulshepherding.org blog.) Willard suggested that it's much more helpful to have periodic extended times of being immersed in God. My suggestion? Make it both-and spend dedicated time with the Father in His word on a daily basis and make time for a day-long or longer retreat to "immerse in God."

8.

RESOURCES

One of the most helpful resources for me as I seek to hear God speak to me through His word is the YouVersion app. This free app, already installed on 405 million unique devices all over the world, currently offers (as of January 24, 2020) 2,035 Bible versions in 1,363 languages! It has no advertising and no in-app purchases, and several of the translations offer audio as well. As I utilize this app, I set up several of my favorite translations (and Eugene Peterson's excellent paraphrase, THE MESSAGE) as those I will compare when I think I am hearing from the Lord. This saves me from interpretive errors, or at least highlights the difficulty of translating certain passages. I thank God for Bobby Gruenewald who created this app in 2007, and for LifeChurch.tv (now Life.Church) and pastor Craig Groeschel who further developed it and who distribute it to the world!

If you would like to understand how God whispers to me on a daily basis, go to hoseabilyeufamily.org and click on Fresh Manna. This audio podcast comes from my heart four or more times each week and is simply the overflow of my 7/24 time that day. If you listen, my hope is that you will say, "Oh, that's how it works! I can do this!"

There is a wealth of resources on the Internet, most of them free, but I would encourage caution as you use them. Always seek to find the theological assumptions anyone brings to their teaching, writing, or blogging. You should be able to find what faith tradition they belong to, and that can give you additional understanding of their biases (and we all have them).

Faithful attendance in a Bible-believing and a Bible-teaching local congregation will be of great help to you as you are learning to hear God's voice in His word. My life has been blessed and changed by the pastors and teachers in churches I have attended through the years. Being in a small group of believers who are also listening regularly to God can give you protection from aberrant thoughts about God and His plan for our lives. Other believers can bring balance to your understanding, and your insights can be helpful to them.

Finally, daily devotionals from the heart of some of God's choice servants (think Charles Spurgeon or Oswald Chambers) have proven helpful to many followers of Christ. However, the "end game" is for you to be able to hear God for yourself, not just feed on pre-digested Word, no matter how tasty! For me, I want to hear for myself **and** benefit from the wisdom of others.

> *So now, brethren* (and sisters!), *I commend you to God and to the word of his grace, which is able to build you up and give you an inheritance among all those who are sanctified* (Acts 20:32 KJV).

ABOUT THE AUTHOR

William Hosea Bilyeu

Hosea Bilyeu is currently the Western Commissioner of Christian County, Missouri, and is serving as the Pastor of The Wells of Joy Church. He is a former mathematics teacher and has served the local church since he was seventeen years old. He served as the full-time pastor of Mt. Sinai Baptist Church near Clever, Missouri, for over five years, and then served as the Senior Pastor of Ridgecrest Baptist Church in Springfield, Missouri, for thirty years. During his years at Ridgecrest God granted 30 years of uninterrupted growth and attendance increasing from twenty-six to two thousand.

Hosea is the author of *The Biblical Preacher's Workshop*; and, with his family, has thirteen Southern Gospel music projects. Hosea and his wife, Debbie, have been married since 1969, and have four children, two awesome sons-in-law, a precious daughter-in-law, six grandchildren, nine great-grandchildren, as well as a "bonus" daughter and granddaughter.

Hosea's primary passion in this season of his life is raising up disciples of Jesus Christ who are grounded in the Word, filled with the Spirit, fierce for the fellowship, and persevering to the end. *The 7/24 Challenge* is central to all of these.

Made in the USA
Coppell, TX
05 July 2022